T0145963

Helen of Troy
and Other Poems

Helen of Troy and Other Poems

Sara Teasdale

MINT EDITIONS

Helen of Troy and Other Poems was first published in 1911.

This edition published by Mint Editions 2021.

ISBN 9781513295930 | E-ISBN 9781513297439

Published by Mint Editions®

 MINT
EDITIONS

minteditionbooks.com

Publishing Director: Jennifer Newens
Design & Production: Rachel Lopez Metzger
Project Manager: Micaela Clark
Typesetting: Westchester Publishing Services

Contents

HELEN OF TROY

Wild flight on flight against the fading dawn
The flames' red wings soar upward duskily.
This is the funeral pyre and Troy is dead
That sparkled so the day I saw it first,
And darkened slowly after. I am she
Who loves all beauty—yet I wither it.
Why have the high gods made me wreak their wrath—
Forever since my maidenhood to sow
Sorrow and blood about me? Lo, they keep
Their bitter care above me even now.
It was the gods who led me to this lair,
That tho' the burning winds should make me weak,
They should not snatch the life from out my lips.
Olympus let the other women die;
They shall be quiet when the day is done
And have no care tomorrow. Yet for me
There is no rest. The gods are not so kind
To her made half immortal like themselves.
It is to you I owe the cruel gift,
Leda, my mother, and the Swan, my sire,
To you the beauty and to you the bale;
For never woman born of man and maid
Had wrought such havoc on the earth as I,
Or troubled heaven with a sea of flame
That climbed to touch the silent whirling stars
And blotted out their brightness ere the dawn.
Have I not made the world to weep enough?
Give death to me. Yet life is more than death;
How could I leave the sound of singing winds,
The strong sweet scent that breathes from off the sea,
Or shut my eyes forever to the spring?
I will not give the grave my hands to hold,
My shining hair to light oblivion.
Have those who wander through the ways of death,
The still wan fields Elysian, any love
To lift their breasts with longing, any lips

To thirst against the quiver of a kiss?
Lo, I shall live to conquer Greece again,
To make the people love, who hate me now.
My dreams are over, I have ceased to cry
Against the fate that made men love my mouth
And left their spirits all too deaf to hear
The little songs that echoed through my soul.
I have no anger now. The dreams are done;
Yet since the Greeks and Trojans would not see
Aught but my body's fairness, till the end,
In all the islands set in all the seas,
And all the lands that lie beneath the sun,
Till light turn darkness, and till time shall sleep,
Men's lives shall waste with longing after me,
For I shall be the sum of their desire,
The whole of beauty, never seen again.
And they shall stretch their arms and starting, wake
With "Helen!" on their lips, and in their eyes
The vision of me. Always I shall be
Limned on the darkness like a shaft of light
That glimmers and is gone. They shall behold
Each one his dream that fashions me anew;—
With hair like lakes that glint beneath the stars
Dark as sweet midnight, or with hair aglow
Like burnished gold that still retains the fire.
Yea, I shall haunt until the dusk of time
The heavy eyelids filled with fleeting dreams.

I wait for one who comes with sword to slay—
The king I wronged who searches for me now;
And yet he shall not slay me. I shall stand
With lifted head and look within his eyes,
Baring my breast to him and to the sun.
He shall not have the power to stain with blood
That whiteness—for the thirsty sword shall fall
And he shall cry and catch me in his arms,
Bearing me back to Sparta on his breast.
Lo, I shall live to conquer Greece again!

SARA TEASDALE

Beatrice

Send out the singers—let the room be still;
They have not eased my pain nor brought me sleep.
Close out the sun, for I would have it dark
That I may feel how black the grave will be.
The sun is setting, for the light is red,
And you are outlined in a golden fire,
Like Ursula upon an altar-screen.
Come, leave the light and sit beside my bed,
For I have had enough of saints and prayers.
Strange broken thoughts are beating in my brain,
They come and vanish and again they come.
It is the fever driving out my soul,
And Death stands waiting by the arras there.

Ornella, I will speak, for soon my lips
Shall keep a silence till the end of time.
You have a mouth for loving—listen then:
Keep tryst with Love before Death comes to tryst;
For I, who die, could wish that I had lived
A little closer to the world of men,
Not watching always thro' the blazoned panes
That show the world in chilly greens and blues
And grudge the sunshine that would enter in.
I was no part of all the troubled crowd
That moved beneath the palace windows here,
And yet sometimes a knight in shining steel
Would pass and catch the gleaming of my hair,
And wave a mailed hand and smile at me,
Whereat I made no sign and turned away,
Affrighted and yet glad and full of dreams.
Ah, dreams and dreams that asked no answering!
I should have wrought to make my dreams come true,
But all my life was like an autumn day,
Full of gray quiet and a hazy peace.

What was I saying? All is gone again.
It seemed but now I was the little child
Who played within a garden long ago.
Beyond the walls the festal trumpets blared.
Perhaps they carried some Madonna by
With tossing ensigns in a sea of flowers,
A painted Virgin with a painted Child,
Who saw for once the sweetness of the sun
Before they shut her in an altar-niche
Where tapers smoke against the windy gloom.
I gathered roses redder than my gown
And played that I was Saint Elizabeth,
Whose wine had turned to roses in her hands.
And as I played, a child came thro' the gate,
A boy who looked at me without a word,
As tho' he saw stretch far behind my head
Long lines of radiant angels, row on row.
That day we spoke a little, timidly,
And after that I never heard the voice
That sang so many songs for love of me.
He was content to stand and watch me pass,
To seek for me at matins everyday,
Where I could feel his eyes the while I prayed.
I think if he had stretched his hands to me,
Or moved his lips to say a single word,
I might have loved him—he had wondrous eyes.

Ornella, are you there? I cannot see—
Is every one so lonely when he dies?

The room is filled with lights—with waving lights—
Who are the men and women 'round the bed?
What have I said, Ornella? Have they heard?
There was no evil hidden in my life,
And yet, and yet, I would not have them know—

Am I not floating in a mist of light?
O lift me up and I shall reach the sun!

SARA TEASDALE

Sappho

The twilight's inner flame grows blue and deep,
And in my Lesbos, over leagues of sea,
The temples glimmer moonwise in the trees.
Twilight has veiled the little flower face
Here on my heart, but still the night is kind
And leaves her warm sweet weight against my breast.
Am I that Sappho who would run at dusk
Along the surges creeping up the shore
When tides came in to ease the hungry beach,
And running, running, till the night was black,
Would fall forespent upon the chilly sand
And quiver with the winds from off the sea?
Ah, quietly the shingle waits the tides
Whose waves are stinging kisses, but to me
Love brought no peace, nor darkness any rest.
I crept and touched the foam with fevered hands
And cried to Love, from whom the sea is sweet,
From whom the sea is bitterer than death.
Ah, Aphrodite, if I sing no more
To thee, God's daughter, powerful as God,
It is that thou hast made my life too sweet
To hold the added sweetness of a song.
There is a quiet at the heart of love,
And I have pierced the pain and come to peace.
I hold my peace, my Cleis, on my heart;
And softer than a little wild bird's wing
Are kisses that she pours upon my mouth.
Ah, never any more when spring like fire
Will flicker in the newly opened leaves,
Shall I steal forth to seek for solitude
Beyond the lure of light Alcaeus' lyre,
Beyond the sob that stilled Erinna's voice.
Ah, never with a throat that aches with song,
Beneath the white uncaring sky of spring,
Shall I go forth to hide awhile from Love
The quiver and the crying of my heart.

Still I remember how I strove to flee
The love-note of the birds, and bowed my head
To hurry faster, but upon the ground
I saw two winged shadows side by side,
And all the world's spring passion stifled me.
Ah, Love, there is no fleeing from thy might,
No lonely place where thou hast never trod,
No desert thou hast left uncarpeted
With flowers that spring beneath thy perfect feet.
In many guises didst thou come to me;
I saw thee by the maidens while they danced,
Phaon allured me with a look of thine,
In Anactoria I knew thy grace,
I looked at Cercolas and saw thine eyes;
But never wholly, soul and body mine,
Didst thou bid any love me as I loved.
Now I have found the peace that fled from me;
Close, close, against my heart I hold my world.
Ah, Love that made my life a lyric cry,
Ah, Love that tuned my lips to lyres of thine,
I taught the world thy music, now alone
I sing for one who falls asleep to hear.

Marianna Alcoforando

(The Portuguese Nun—1640–1723)

The sparrows wake beneath the convent eaves;
I think I have not slept the whole night through.
But I am old; the aged scarcely know
The times they wake and sleep, for life burns down;
They breathe the calm of death before they die.
The long night ends, the day comes creeping in,
Showing the sorrows that the darkness hid,
The bended head of Christ, the blood, the thorns,
The wall's gray stains of damp, the pallet bed
Where little Sister Marta dreams of saints,
Waking with arms outstretched imploringly
That seek to stay a vision's vanishing.
I never had a vision, yet for me
Our Lady smiled while all the convent slept
One winter midnight hushed around with snow—
I thought she might be kinder than the rest,
And so I came to kneel before her feet,
Sick with love's sorrow and love's bitterness.
But when I would have made the blessed sign,
I found the water frozen in the font,
And touched but ice within the carved stone.
The saints had hid themselves away from me,
Leaving the windows black against the night;
And when I sank upon the altar steps,
Before the Virgin Mother and her Child,
The last, pale, low-burnt taper flickered out,
But in the darkness, smooth and fathomless,
Still twinkled like a star the holy lamp
That cast a dusky glow upon her face.
Then through the numbing cold peace fell on me,
Submission and the gracious gift of tears,
For when I looked, Oh! blessed miracle,
Her lips had parted and Our Lady smiled!
And then I knew that Love is worth its pain

And that my heart was richer for his sake,
Since lack of love is bitterest of all.

The day is broad awake—the first long beam
Of level sun finds Sister Marta's face,
And trembling there it lights a timid smile
Upon the lips that say so many prayers,
And have no words for hate and none for love.
But when she passes where her prayers have gone,
Will God not smile a little sadly then,
And send her back with gentle words to earth
That she may hold a child against her breast
And feel its little hands upon her hair?
We weep before the Blessed Mother's shrine,
To think upon her sorrows, but her joys
What nun could ever know a tithing of?
The precious hours she watched above His sleep
Were worth the fearful anguish of the end.
Yea, lack of love is bitterest of all;
Yet I have felt what thing it is to know
One thought forever, sleeping or awake;
To say one name whose sweetness grows so strange
That it might work a spell on those who weep;
To feel the weight of love upon my heart
So heavy that the blood can scarcely flow.
Love comes to some unlooked-for, quietly,
As when at twilight, with a soft surprise,
We see the new-born crescent in the blue;
And unto others love is planet-like,
A cold and placid gleam that wavers not,
And there are those who wait the call of love
Expectant of his coming, as we watch
To see the east grow pallid ere the moon
Lifts up her flower-like head against the night.
Love came to me as comes a cruel sun,
That on some rain-drenched morning, when the leaves
Are bowed beneath their clinging weight of drops,
Tears through the mist, and burns with fervent heat
The tender grasses and the meadow flowers;

Then suddenly the heavy clouds close in
And through the dark the thunder's muttering
Is drowned amid the dashing of the rain.

But I have seen my day grow calm again.
The sun sets slowly on a peaceful world,
And sheds a quiet light across the fields.

GUENEVERE

I was a queen, and I have lost my crown;
A wife, and I have broken all my vows;
A lover, and I ruined him I loved:—
There is no other havoc left to do.
A little month ago I was a queen,
And mothers held their babies up to see
When I came riding out of Camelot.
The women smiled, and all the world smiled too.
And now, what woman's eyes would smile on me?
I still am beautiful, and yet what child
Would think of me as some high, heaven-sent thing,
An angel, clad in gold and miniver?
The world would run from me, and yet am I
No different from the queen they used to love.
If water, flowing silver over stones,
Is forded, and beneath the horses' feet
Grows turbid suddenly, it clears again,
And men will drink it with no thought of harm.
Yet I am branded for a single fault.

I was the flower amid a toiling world,
Where people smiled to see one happy thing,
And they were proud and glad to raise me high;
They only asked that I should be right fair,
A little kind, and gowned wondrously,
And surely it were little praise to me
If I had pleased them well throughout my life.

I was a queen, the daughter of a king.
The crown was never heavy on my head,
It was my right, and was a part of me.
The women thought me proud, the men were kind,
And bowed right gallantly to kiss my hand,
And watched me as I passed them calmly by,
Along the halls I shall not tread again.
What if, tonight, I should revisit them?

The warders at the gates, the kitchen-maids,
The very beggars would stand off from me,
And I, their queen, would climb the stairs alone,
Pass through the banquet-hall, a loathed thing,
And seek my chambers for a hiding-place,
And I should find them but a sepulchre,
The very rushes rotted on the floors,
The fire in ashes on the freezing hearth.
I was a queen, and he who loved me best
Made me a woman for a night and day,
And now I go unqueened forevermore.
A queen should never dream on summer eves,
When hovering spells are heavy in the dusk:—
I think no night was ever quite so still,
So smoothly lit with red along the west,
So deeply hushed with quiet through and through.
And strangely clear, and deeply dyed with light,
The trees stood straight against a paling sky,
With Venus burning lamp-like in the west.

I walked alone amid a thousand flowers,
That drooped their heads and drowsed beneath the dew,
And all my thoughts were quieted to sleep.
Behind me, on the walk, I heard a step—
I did not know my heart could tell his tread,
I did not know I loved him till that hour.
Within my breast I felt a wild, sick pain,
The garden reeled a little, I was weak,
And quick he came behind me, caught my arms,
That ached beneath his touch; and then I swayed,
My head fell backward and I saw his face.

All this grows bitter that was once so sweet,
And many mouths must drain the dregs of it.
But none will pity me, nor pity him
Whom Love so lashed, and with such cruel thongs.

Erinna

They sent you in to say farewell to me,
No, do not shake your head; I see your eyes
That shine with tears. Sappho, you saw the sun
Just now when you came hither, and again,
When you have left me, all the shimmering
Great meadows will laugh lightly, and the sun
Put round about you warm invisible arms
As might a lover, decking you with light.
I go toward darkness tho' I lie so still.
If I could see the sun, I should look up
And drink the light until my eyes were blind;
I should kneel down and kiss the blades of grass,
And I should call the birds with such a voice,
With such a longing, tremulous and keen,
That they would fly to me and on the breast
Bear evermore to tree-tops and to fields
The kiss I gave them. Sappho, tell me this,
Was I not sometimes fair? My eyes, my mouth,
My hair that loved the wind, were they not worth
The breath of love upon them? Yet he passed,
And he will pass tonight when all the air
Is blue with twilight; but I shall not see.
I shall have gone forever. Hold my hands,
Hold fast that Death may never come between;
Swear by the gods you will not let me go;
Make songs for Death as you would sing to Love—
But you will not assuage him. He alone
Of all the gods will take no gifts from men.
I am afraid, afraid.

                    Sappho, lean down.
Last night the fever gave a dream to me,
It takes my life and gives a little dream.
I thought I saw him stand, the man I love,
Here in my quiet chamber, with his eyes
Fixed on me as I entered, while he drew

Silently toward me—he who night by night
Goes by my door without a thought of me—
Neared me and put his hand behind my head,
And leaning toward me, kissed me on the mouth.
That was a little dream for Death to give,
Too short to take the whole of life for, yet
I woke with lips made quiet by a kiss.
The dream is worth the dying. Do not smile
So sadly on me with your shining eyes,
You who can set your sorrow to a song
And ease your hurt by singing. But to me
My songs are less than sea-sand that the wind
Drives stinging over me and bears away.
I have no care what place the grains may fall,
Nor of my songs, if Time shall blow them back,
As land-wind breaks the lines of dying foam
Along the bright wet beaches, scattering
The flakes once more against the laboring sea,
Into oblivion. What care have I
To please Apollo since Love hearkens not?
Your words will live forever, men will say
"She was the perfect lover"—I shall die,
I loved too much to live. Go Sappho, go—
I hate your hands that beat so full of life,
Go, lest my hatred hurt you. I shall die,
But you will live to love and love again.
He might have loved some other spring than this;
I should have kept my life—I let it go.
He would not love me now tho' Cypris bound
Her girdle round me. I am Death's, not Love's.
Go from me, Sappho, back to find the sun.

I am alone, alone. O Cyprian. . .

LOVE SONGS

Song

You bound strong sandals on my feet,
    You gave me bread and wine,
And bade me out, 'neath sun and stars,
    For all the world was mine.

Oh take the sandals off my feet,
    You know not what you do;
For all my world is in your arms,
    My sun and stars are you.

The Rose and the Bee

If I were a bee and you were a rose,
Would you let me in when the gray wind blows?
Would you hold your petals wide apart,
Would you let me in to find your heart,
        If you were a rose?

"If I were a rose and you were a bee,
You should never go when you came to me,
I should hold my love on my heart at last,
I should close my leaves and keep you fast,
        If you were a bee."

The Song Maker

I made a hundred little songs
    That told the joy and pain of love,
And sang them blithely, tho' I knew
    No whit thereof.

I was a weaver deaf and blind;
    A miracle was wrought for me,
But I have lost my skill to weave
    Since I can see.

For while I sang—ah swift and strange!
    Love passed and touched me on the brow,
And I who made so many songs
    Am silent now.

WILD ASTERS

In the spring I asked the daisies
    If his words were true,
And the clever little daisies
    Always knew.

Now the fields are brown and barren,
    Bitter autumn blows,
And of all the stupid asters
    Not one knows.

WHEN LOVE GOES

I

O mother, I am sick of love,
    I cannot laugh nor lift my head,
My bitter dreams have broken me,
    I would my love were dead.

"Drink of the draught I brew for thee,
Thou shalt have quiet in its stead."

II

Where is the silver in the rain,
    Where is the music in the sea,
Where is the bird that sang all day
    To break my heart with melody?

"The night thou badst Love fly away,
He hid them all from thee."

The Wayfarer

Love entered in my heart one day,
    A sad, unwelcome guest;
But when he begged that he might stay,
    I let him wait and rest.

He broke my sleep with sorrowing,
    And shook my dreams with tears,
And when my heart was fain to sing,
    He stilled its joy with fears.

But now that he has gone his way,
    I miss the old sweet pain,
And sometimes in the night I pray
    That he may come again.

The Princess in the Tower

I

The Princess sings:

I am the princess up in the tower
 And I dream the whole day thro'
Of a knight who shall come with a silver spear
 And a waving plume of blue.

I am the princess up in the tower,
 And I dream my dreams by day,
But sometimes I wake, and my eyes are wet,
 When the dusk is deep and gray.

For the peasant lovers go by beneath,
 I hear them laugh and kiss,
And I forget my day-dream knight,
 And long for a love like this.

II

The Minstrel sings:

I lie beside the princess' tower,
 So close she cannot see my face,
And watch her dreaming all day long,
 And bending with a lily's grace.

Her cheeks are paler than the moon
 That sails along a sunny sky,
And yet her silent mouth is red
 Where tender words and kisses lie.

I am a minstrel with a harp,
 For love of her my songs are sweet,
And yet I dare not lift the voice
 That lies so far beneath her feet.

III

The Knight sings:

O princess cease your dreams awhile
    And look adown your tower's gray side—
The princess gazes far away,
    Nor hears nor heeds the words I cried.

Perchance my heart was overbold,
    God made her dreams too pure to break,
She sees the angels in the air
    Fly to and fro for Mary's sake.

Farewell, I mount and go my way,
    —But oh her hair the sun sifts thro'—
The tilts and tourneys wait my spear,
    I am the Knight of the Plume of Blue.

WHEN LOVE WAS BORN

When Love was born I think he lay
    Right warm on Venus' breast,
And whiles he smiled and whiles would play
    And whiles would take his rest.

But always, folded out of sight,
    The wings were growing strong
That were to bear him off in flight
    Erelong, erelong.

The Shrine

There is no lord within my heart,
    Left silent as an empty shrine
    Where rose and myrtle intertwine,
Within a place apart.

No god is there of carven stone
    To watch with still approving eyes
    My thoughts like steady incense rise;
I dream and weep alone.

But if I keep my altar fair,
    Some morning I shall lift my head
    From roses deftly garlanded
To find the god is there.

THE BLIND

The birds are all a-building,
    They say the world's a-flower,
And still I linger lonely
    Within a barren bower.

I weave a web of fancies
    Of tears and darkness spun.
How shall I sing of sunlight
    Who never saw the sun?

I hear the pipes a-blowing,
    But yet I may not dance,
I know that Love is passing,
    I cannot catch his glance.

And if his voice should call me
    And I with groping dim
Should reach his place of calling
    And stretch my arms to him,

The wind would blow between my hands
    For Joy that I shall miss,
The rain would fall upon my mouth
    That his will never kiss.

LOVE ME

Brown-thrush singing all day long
    In the leaves above me,
Take my love this little song,
    "Love me, love me, love me!"

When he harkens what you say,
    Bid him, lest he miss me,
Leave his work or leave his play,
    And kiss me, kiss me, kiss me!

The Song for Colin

I sang a song at dusking time
    Beneath the evening star,
And Terence left his latest rhyme
    To answer from afar.

Pierrot laid down his lute to weep,
    And sighed, "She sings for me,"
But Colin slept a careless sleep
    Beneath an apple tree.

Four Winds

"Four winds blowing thro' the sky,
You have seen poor maidens die,
Tell me then what I shall do
That my lover may be true."
Said the wind from out the south,
"Lay no kiss upon his mouth,"
And the wind from out the west,
"Wound the heart within his breast,"
And the wind from out the east,
"Send him empty from the feast,"
And the wind from out the north,
"In the tempest thrust him forth,
When thou art more cruel than he,
Then will Love be kind to thee."

Roundel

If he could know my songs are all for him,
At silver dawn or in the evening glow,
Would he not smile and think it but a whim,
        If he could know?

Or would his heart rejoice and overflow,
As happy brooks that break their icy rim
When April's horns along the hillsides blow?

I may not speak till Eros' torch is dim,
The god is bitter and will have it so;
And yet tonight our fate would seem less grim
        If he could know.

DEW

I dream that he is mine,
  I dream that he is true,
And all his words I keep
  As rose-leaves hold the dew.

O little thirsty rose,
  O little heart beware,
Lest you should hope to hold
  A hundred roses' share.

A Maiden

Oh if I were the velvet rose
    Upon the red rose vine,
I'd climb to touch his window
    And make his casement fine.

And if I were the little bird
    That twitters on the tree,
All day I'd sing my love for him
    Till he should harken me.

But since I am a maiden
    I go with downcast eyes,
And he will never hear the songs
    That he has turned to sighs.

And since I am a maiden
    My love will never know
That I could kiss him with a mouth
    More red than roses blow.

"I Love You"

When April bends above me
    And finds me fast asleep,
Dust need not keep the secret
    A live heart died to keep.

When April tells the thrushes,
    The meadow-larks will know,
And pipe the three words lightly
    To all the winds that blow.

Above his roof the swallows,
    In notes like far-blown rain,
Will tell the little sparrow
    Beside his window-pane.

O sparrow, little sparrow,
    When I am fast asleep,
Then tell my love the secret
    That I have died to keep.

But Not to Me

The April night is still and sweet
    With flowers on every tree;
Peace comes to them on quiet feet,
       But not to me.

My peace is hidden in his breast
    Where I shall never be,
Love comes tonight to all the rest,
       But not to me.

HIDDEN LOVE

I hid the love within my heart,
    And lit the laughter in my eyes,
That when we meet he may not know
    My love that never dies.

But sometimes when he dreams at night
    Of fragrant forests green and dim,
It may be that my love crept out
    And brought the dream to him.

And sometimes when his heart is sick
    And suddenly grows well again,
It may be that my love was there
    To free his life of pain.

SNOW SONG

Fairy snow, fairy snow,
Blowing, blowing everywhere,
    Would that I
    Too, could fly
Lightly, lightly through the air.

Like a wee, crystal star
I should drift, I should blow
    Near, more near,
    To my dear
Where he comes through the snow.

I should fly to my love
Like a flake in the storm,
    I should die,
    I should die,
On his lips that are warm.

Youth and the Pilgrim

Gray pilgrim, you have journeyed far,
    I pray you tell to me
Is there a land where Love is not,
    By shore of any sea?

For I am weary of the god,
    And I would flee from him
Tho' I must take a ship and go
    Beyond the ocean's rim.

"I know a port where Love is not,
    The ship is in your hand,
Then plunge your sword within your breast
    And you will reach the land."

The Wanderer

I saw the sunset-colored sands,
    The Nile like flowing fire between,
    Where Rameses stares forth serene,
And Ammon's heavy temple stands.

I saw the rocks where long ago,
    Above the sea that cries and breaks,
    Bright Perseus with Medusa's snakes
Set free the maiden white like snow.

And many skies have covered me,
    And many winds have blown me forth,
    And I have loved the green bright north,
And I have loved the cold sweet sea.

But what to me are north and south,
    And what the lure of many lands,
    Since you have leaned to catch my hands
And lay a kiss upon my mouth.

I Would Live in Your Love

I would live in your love as the sea-grasses live in the sea,
Borne up by each wave as it passes, drawn down by each wave that
recedes;
I would empty my soul of the dreams that have gathered in me,
I would beat with your heart as it beats, I would follow your soul as it
leads.

MAY

The wind is tossing the lilacs,
    The new leaves laugh in the sun,
And the petals fall on the orchard wall,
    But for me the spring is done.

Beneath the apple blossoms
    I go a wintry way,
For love that smiled in April
    Is false to me in May.

Rispetto

Was that his step that sounded on the stair?
    Was that his knock I heard upon the door?
I grow so tired I almost cease to care,
    And yet I would that he might come once more.

It was the wind I heard, that mocks at me,
The bitter wind that is more cruel than he;
It was the wind that knocked upon the door,
But he will never knock nor enter more.

Less than the Cloud to the Wind

Less than the cloud to the wind,
　　Less than the foam to the sea,
Less than the rose to the storm
　　　Am I to thee.

More than the star to the night,
　　More than the rain to the lea,
More than heaven to earth
　　　Art thou to me.

BURIED LOVE

I shall bury my weary Love
    Beneath a tree,
In the forest tall and black
    Where none can see.

I shall put no flowers at his head,
    Nor stone at his feet,
For the mouth I loved so much
    Was bittersweet.

I shall go no more to his grave,
    For the woods are cold.
I shall gather as much of joy
    As my hands can hold.

I shall stay all day in the sun
    Where the wide winds blow,
But oh, I shall weep at night
    When none will know.

Song

O woe is me, my heart is sad,
    For I should never know
If Love came by like any lad,
    Without his silver bow.

Or if he left his arrows sharp
    And came a minstrel weary,
I'd never tell him by his harp
    Nor know him for my dearie.

"O go your ways and have no fear,
    For tho' Love passes by,
He'll come a hundred times, my dear,
    Before your turn to die."

Pierrot

Pierrot stands in the garden
    Beneath a waning moon,
And on his lute he fashions
    A little silver tune.

Pierrot plays in the garden,
    He thinks he plays for me,
But I am quite forgotten
    Under the cherry tree.

Pierrot plays in the garden,
    And all the roses know
That Pierrot loves his music,
    But I love Pierrot.

At Night

Love said, "Wake still and think of me,"
    Sleep, "Close your eyes till break of day,"
But Dreams came by and smilingly
    Gave both to Love and Sleep their way.

Song

When Love comes singing to his heart
    That would not wake for me,
I think that I shall know his joy
    By my own ecstasy.

And tho' the sea were all between,
    The time their hands shall meet,
My heart will know his happiness,
    So wildly it will beat.

And when he bends above her mouth,
    Rejoicing for his sake,
My soul will sing a little song,
    But oh, my heart will break.

Love in Autumn

I sought among the drifting leaves,
    The golden leaves that once were green,
To see if Love were hiding there
    And peeping out between.

For thro' the silver showers of May
    And thro' the summer's heavy heat,
In vain I sought his golden head
    And light, fast-flying feet.

Perhaps when all the world is bare
    And cruel winter holds the land,
The Love that finds no place to hide
    Will run and catch my hand.

I shall not care to have him then,
    I shall be bitter and a-cold—
It grows too late for frolicking
    When all the world is old.

Then little hiding Love, come forth,
    Come forth before the autumn goes,
And let us seek thro' ruined paths
    The garden's last red rose.

The Kiss

I hoped that he would love me,
    And he has kissed my mouth,
But I am like a stricken bird
    That cannot reach the south.

For tho' I know he loves me,
    Tonight my heart is sad;
His kiss was not so wonderful
    As all the dreams I had.

November

The world is tired, the year is old,
    The little leaves are glad to die,
The wind goes shivering with cold
    Among the rushes dry.

Our love is dying like the grass,
    And we who kissed grow coldly kind,
Half glad to see our poor love pass
    Like leaves along the wind.

A Song of the Princess

The princess has her lovers,
    A score of knights has she,
And each can sing a madrigal,
    And praise her gracefully.

But Love that is so bitter
    Hath put within her heart
A longing for the scornful knight
    Who silent stands apart.

And tho' the others praise and plead,
    She maketh no reply,
Yet for a single word from him,
    I ween that she would die.

The Wind

A wind is blowing over my soul,
    I hear it cry the whole night thro'—
Is there no peace for me on earth
    Except with you?

Alas, the wind has made me wise,
    Over my naked soul it blew,—
There is no peace for me on earth
    Even with you.

A Winter Night

My window-pane is starred with frost,
    The world is bitter cold tonight,
The moon is cruel and the wind
    Is like a two-edged sword to smite.

God pity all the homeless ones,
    The beggars pacing to and fro.
God pity all the poor tonight
    Who walk the lamp-lit streets of snow.

My room is like a bit of June,
    Warm and close-curtained fold on fold,
But somewhere, like a homeless child,
    My heart is crying in the cold.

The Metropolitan Tower

We walked together in the dusk
　　To watch the tower grow dimly white,
And saw it lift against the sky
　　Its flower of amber light.

You talked of half a hundred things,
　　I kept each little word you said;
And when at last the hour was full,
　　I saw the light turn red.

You did not know the time had come,
　　You did not see the sudden flower,
Nor know that in my heart Love's birth
　　Was reckoned from that hour.

Gramercy Park

For W. P.

The little park was filled with peace,
    The walks were carpeted with snow,
But every iron gate was locked.
    Lest if we entered, peace would go.

We circled it a dozen times,
    The wind was blowing from the sea,
I only felt your restless eyes
    Whose love was like a cloak for me.

Oh heavy gates that fate has locked
    To bar the joy we may not win,
Peace would go out forevermore
    If we should dare to enter in.

In the Metropolitan Museum

Within the tiny Pantheon
    We stood together silently,
Leaving the restless crowd awhile
    As ships find shelter from the sea.

The ancient centuries came back
    To cover us a moment's space,
And thro' the dome the light was glad
    Because it shone upon your face.

Ah, not from Rome but farther still,
    Beyond sun-smitten Salamis,
The moment took us, till you stooped
    To find the present with a kiss.

CONEY ISLAND

Why did you bring me here?
The sand is white with snow,
Over the wooden domes
The winter sea-winds blow—
There is no shelter near,
    Come, let us go.

With foam of icy lace
The sea creeps up the sand,
The wind is like a hand
That strikes us in the face.
Doors that June set a-swing
Are bolted long ago;
We try them uselessly—
Alas, there cannot be
For us a second spring;
    Come, let us go.

UNION SQUARE

With the man I love who loves me not,
    I walked in the street-lamps' flare;
We watched the world go home that night
    In a flood through Union Square.

I leaned to catch the words he said
    That were light as a snowflake falling;
Ah well that he never leaned to hear
    The words my heart was calling.

And on we walked and on we walked
    Past the fiery lights of the picture shows—
Where the girls with thirsty eyes go by
    On the errand each man knows.

And on we walked and on we walked,
    At the door at last we said good-bye;
I knew by his smile he had not heard
    My heart's unuttered cry.

With the man I love who loves me not
    I walked in the street-lamps' flare—
But oh, the girls who can ask for love
    In the lights of Union Square.

Central Park at Dusk

Buildings above the leafless trees
    Loom high as castles in a dream,
While one by one the lamps come out
    To thread the twilight with a gleam.

There is no sign of leaf or bud,
    A hush is over everything—
Silent as women wait for love,
    The world is waiting for the spring.

Young Love

I

I cannot heed the words they say,
    The lights grow far away and dim,
Amid the laughing men and maids
    My eyes unbidden seek for him.

I hope that when he smiles at me
    He does not guess my joy and pain,
For if he did, he is too kind
    To ever look my way again.

II

I have a secret in my heart
    No ears have ever heard,
And still it sings there day by day
    Most like a caged bird.

And when it beats against the bars,
    I do not set it free,
For I am happier to know
    It only sings for me.

III

I wrote his name along the beach,
    I love the letters so.
Far up it seemed and out of reach,
    For still the tide was low.

But oh, the sea came creeping up,
    And washed the name away,
And on the sand where it had been
    A bit of sea-grass lay.

A bit of sea-grass on the sand,
    Dropped from a mermaid's hair—
Ah, had she come to kiss his name
    And leave a token there?

IV

What am I that he should love me,
He who stands so far above me,
    What am I?
I am like a cowslip turning
    Toward the sky,
Where a planet's golden burning
Breaks the cowslip's heart with yearning,
What am I that he should love me,
    What am I?

V

O dreams that flock about my sleep,
    I pray you bring my love to me,
And let me think I hear his voice
    Again ring free.

And if you care to please me well,
    And live tomorrow in my mind,
Let him who was so cold before,
    Tonight seem kind.

VI

I plucked a daisy in the fields,
    And there beneath the sun
I let its silver petals fall
        One after one.

I said, "He loves me, loves me not,"
    And oh, my heart beat fast,

SARA TEASDALE

The flower was kind, it let me say
    "He loves me," last.

I kissed the little leafless stem,
    But oh, my poor heart knew
The words the flower had said to me,
    They were not true.

VII

I sent my love a letter,
    And if he loves me not,
He shall not find my love for him
    In any line or dot.

But if he loves me truly,
    He'll find it hidden deep,
As dawn gleams red thro' chilly clouds
    To eyes awaked from sleep.

VIII

The world is cold and gray and wet,
And I am heavy-hearted, yet
When I am home and look to see
The place my letters wait for me,
If I should find ONE letter there,
I think I should not greatly care
If it were rainy or were fair,
For all the world would suddenly
Seem like a festival to me.

IX

I hid three words within my heart,
    That longed to fly to him,
At dawn they woke me with a start,
    They sang till day was dim.

And now at last I let them fly,
    As little birds should do,
And he will know the first is "I,"
    The others "Love" and "You."

X

Across the twilight's violet
    His curtained window glimmers gold;
Oh happy light that round my love
      Can fold.

Oh happy book within his hand,
    Oh happy page he glorifies,
Oh happy little word beneath
      His eyes.

But oh, thrice happy, happy I
    Who love him more than songs can tell,
For in the heaven of his heart
      I dwell.

SONNETS AND LYRICS

Primavera Mia

As kings who see their little life-day pass,
Take off the heavy ermine and the crown,
So had the trees that autumn-time laid down
Their golden garments on the faded grass,
When I, who watched the seasons in the glass
Of mine own thoughts, saw all the autumn's brown
Leap into life and don a sunny gown
Of leafage such as happy April has.
Great spring came singing upward from the south;
For in my heart, far carried on the wind,
Your words like winged seeds took root and grew,
And all the world caught music from your mouth;
I saw the light as one who had been blind,
And knew my sun and song and spring were you.

Soul's Birth

When you were born, beloved, was your soul
New made by God to match your body's flower,
And were they both at one same precious hour
Sent forth from heaven as a perfect whole?
Or had your soul since dim creation burned,
A star in some still region of the sky,
That leaping earthward, left its place on high
And to your little new-born body yearned?
No words can tell in what celestial hour
God made your soul and gave it mortal birth,
Nor in the disarray of all the stars
Is any place so sweet that such a flower
Might linger there until thro' heaven's bars,
It heard God's voice that bade it down to earth.

Love and Death

Shall we, too, rise forgetful from our sleep,
And shall my soul that lies within your hand
Remember nothing, as the blowing sand
Forgets the palm where long blue shadows creep
When winds along the darkened desert sweep?
Or would it still remember, tho' it spanned
A thousand heavens, while the planets fanned
The vacant ether with their voices deep?
Soul of my soul, no word shall be forgot,
Nor yet alone, beloved, shall we see
The desolation of extinguished suns,
Nor fear the void wherethro' our planet runs,
For still together shall we go and not
Fare forth alone to front eternity.

FOR THE ANNIVERSARY OF JOHN KEATS' DEATH

(February 23, 1821)

At midnight when the moonlit cypress trees
Have woven round his grave a magic shade,
Still weeping the unfinished hymn he made,
There moves fresh Maia like a morning breeze
Blown over jonquil beds when warm rains cease.
And stooping where her poet's head is laid,
Selene weeps while all the tides are stayed
And swaying seas are darkened into peace.
But they who wake the meadows and the tides
Have hearts too kind to bid him wake from sleep
Who murmurs sometimes when his dreams are deep,
Startling the Quiet Land where he abides,
And charming still, sad-eyed Persephone
With visions of the sunny earth and sea.

SILENCE

(To Eleonora Duse)

We are anhungered after solitude,
Deep stillness pure of any speech or sound,
Soft quiet hovering over pools profound,
The silences that on the desert brood,
Above a windless hush of empty seas,
The broad unfurling banners of the dawn,
A faery forest where there sleeps a Faun;
Our souls are fain of solitudes like these.
O woman who divined our weariness,
And set the crown of silence on your art,
From what undreamed-of depth within your heart
Have you sent forth the hush that makes us free
To hear an instant, high above earth's stress,
The silent music of infinity?

The Return

I turned the key and opened wide the door
To enter my deserted room again,
Where thro' the long hot months the dust had lain.
Was it not lonely when across the floor
No step was heard, no sudden song that bore
My whole heart upward with a joyous pain?
Were not the pictures and the volumes fain
To have me with them always as before?
But Giorgione's Venus did not deign
To lift her lids, nor did the subtle smile
Of Mona Lisa deepen. Madeleine
Still wept against the glory of her hair,
Nor did the lovers part their lips the while,
But kissed unheeding that I watched them there.

FEAR

I am afraid, oh I am so afraid!
The cold black fear is clutching me tonight
As long ago when they would take the light
And leave the little child who would have prayed,
Frozen and sleepless at the thought of death.
My heart that beats too fast will rest too soon;
I shall not know if it be night or noon,—
Yet shall I struggle in the dark for breath?
Will no one fight the Terror for my sake,
The heavy darkness that no dawn will break?
How can they leave me in that dark alone,
Who loved the joy of light and warmth so much,
And thrilled so with the sense of sound and touch,—
How can they shut me underneath a stone?

ANADYOMENE

The wide, bright temple of the world I found,
And entered from the dizzy infinite
That I might kneel and worship thee in it;
Leaving the singing stars their ceaseless round
Of silver music sound on orbed sound,
For measured spaces where the shrines are lit,
And men with wisdom or with little wit
Implore the gods that mercy may abound.
Ah, Aphrodite, was it not from thee
My summons came across the endless spaces?
Mother of Love, turn not thy face from me
Now that I seek for thee in human faces;
Answer my prayer or set my spirit free
Again to drift along the starry places.

Galahad in the Castle of the Maidens

(To the maiden with the hidden face in Abbey's painting)

The other maidens raised their eyes to him
Who stumbled in before them when the fight
Had left him victor, with a victor's right.
I think his eyes with quick hot tears grew dim;
He scarcely saw her swaying white and slim,
And trembling slightly, dreaming of his might,
Nor knew he touched her hand, as strangely light
As a wan wraith's beside a river's rim.
The other maidens raised their eyes to see
And only she has hid her face away,
And yet I ween she loved him more than they,
And very fairly fashioned was her face.
Yet for Love's shame and sweet humility,
She dared not meet him with their queenlike grace.

To an Aeolian Harp

The winds have grown articulate in thee,
And voiced again the wail of ancient woe
That smote upon the winds of long ago:
The cries of Trojan women as they flee,
The quivering moan of pale Andromache,
Now lifted loud with pain and now brought low.
It is the soul of sorrow that we know,
As in a shell the soul of all the sea.
So sometimes in the compass of a song,
Unknown to him who sings, thro' lips that live,
The voiceless dead of long-forgotten lands
Proclaim to us their heaviness and wrong
In sweeping sadness of the winds that give
Thy strings no rest from weariless wild hands.

To Erinna

Was Time not harsh to you, or was he kind,
O pale Erinna of the perfect lyre,
That he has left no word of singing fire
Whereby you waked the dreaming Lesbian wind,
And kindled night along the lyric shore?
O girl whose lips Erato stooped to kiss,
Do you go sorrowing because of this
In fields where poets sing forevermore?
Or are you glad and is it best to be
A silent music men have never heard,
A dream in all our souls that we may say:
"Her voice had all the rapture of the sea,
And all the clear cool quiver of a bird
Deep in a forest at the break of day"?

To Cleis

"I have a fair daughter with a form like a golden flower, Cleis, the beloved."

—Sapphic fragment

When the dusk was wet with dew,
    Cleis, did the muses nine
    Listen in a silent line
While your mother sang to you?

Did they weep or did they smile
    When she crooned to still your cries,
    She, a muse in human guise,
Who forsook her lyre awhile?

Did you feel her wild heart beat?
    Did the warmth of all the sun
    Thro' your little body run
When she kissed your hands and feet?

Did your fingers, babywise,
    Touch her face and touch her hair,
    Did you think your mother fair,
Could you bear her burning eyes?

Are the songs that soothed your fears
    Vanished like a vanished flame,
    Save the line where shines your name
Starlike down the graying years?

Cleis speaks no word to me,
    For the land where she has gone
    Lieth mute at dusk and dawn
Like a windless tideless sea.

Paris in Spring

The city's all a-shining
    Beneath a fickle sun,
A gay young wind's a-blowing,
    The little shower is done.
But the rain-drops still are clinging
    And falling one by one—
Oh it's Paris, it's Paris,
    And spring-time has begun.

I know the Bois is twinkling
    In a sort of hazy sheen,
And down the Champs the gray old arch
    Stands cold and still between.
But the walk is flecked with sunlight
    Where the great acacias lean,
Oh it's Paris, it's Paris,
    And the leaves are growing green.

The sun's gone in, the sparkle's dead,
    There falls a dash of rain,
But who would care when such an air
    Comes blowing up the Seine?
And still Ninette sits sewing
    Beside her window-pane,
When it's Paris, it's Paris,
    And spring-time's come again.

Madeira from the Sea

Out of the delicate dream of the distance an emerald emerges
Veiled in the violet folds of the air of the sea;
Softly the dream grows awakening—shimmering white of a city,
Splashes of crimson, the gay bougainvillea, the palms.
High in the infinite blue of its heaven a quiet cloud lingers,
Lost and forgotten of winds that have fallen asleep,
Fallen asleep to the tune of a Portuguese song in a garden.

CITY VIGNETTES

I

Dawn

The greenish sky glows up in misty reds,
    The purple shadows turn to brick and stone,
The dreams wear thin, men turn upon their beds,
    And hear the milk-cart jangle by alone.

II

Dusk

The city's street, a roaring blackened stream
    Walled in by granite, thro' whose thousand eyes
A thousand yellow lights begin to gleam,
    And over all the pale untroubled skies.

III

Rain at Night

The street-lamps shine in a yellow line
    Down the splashy, gleaming street,
And the rain is heard now loud now blurred
    By the tread of homing feet.

By the Sea

Beside an ebbing northern sea
While stars awaken one by one,
We walk together, I and he.

He woos me with an easy grace
That proves him only half sincere;
A light smile flickers on his face.

To him love-making is an art,
And as a flutist plays a flute,
So does he play upon his heart

A music varied to his whim.
He has no use for love of mine,
He would not have me answer him.

To hide my eyes within the night
I watch the changeful lighthouse gleam
Alternately with red and white.

My laughter smites upon my ears,
So one who cries and wakes from sleep
Knows not it is himself he hears.

What if my voice should let him know
The mocking words were all a sham,
And lips that laugh could tremble so?

What if I lost the power to lie,
And he should only hear his name
In one low, broken cry?

On the Death of Swinburne

He trod the earth but yesterday,
And now he treads the stars.
    He left us in the April time
    He praised so often in his rhyme,
He left the singing and the lyre and went his way.

He drew new music from our tongue,
A music subtly wrought,
    And moulded words to his desire,
    As wind doth mould a wave of fire;
From strangely fashioned harps slow golden tones he wrung.

I think the singing understands
That he who sang is still,
    And Iseult cries that he is dead,—
    Does not Dolores bow her head
And Fragoletta weep and wring her little hands?

New singing now the singer hears
To lyre and lute and harp;
    Catullus waits to welcome him,
    And thro' the twilight sweet and dim,
Sappho's forgotten songs are falling on his ears.

TRIOLETS

I

Love looked back as he took his flight,
    And lo, his eyes were filled with tears.
Was it for love of lost delight
Love looked back as he took his flight?
Only I know while day grew night,
    Turning still to the vanished years,
Love looked back as he took his flight,
    And lo, his eyes were filled with tears.

II

(Written in a copy of "La Vita Nuova." For M. C. S.)

If you were Lady Beatrice
    And I the Florentine,
I'd never waste my time like this—
If you were Lady Beatrice
I'd woo and then demand a kiss,
    Nor weep like Dante here, I ween,
If you were Lady Beatrice
    And I the Florentine.

III

(Written in a copy of "The Poems of Sappho.")

Beyond the dim Hesperides,
    The girl who sang them long ago
Could never dream that over seas,
Beyond the dim Hesperides,
The wind would blow such songs as these—
    I wonder now if she can know,
Beyond the dim Hesperides,
    The girl who sang them long ago?

IV

Dead leaves upon the stream
    And dead leaves on the air—
All of my lost hopes seem
Dead leaves upon the stream;
I watch them in a dream,
    Going I know not where,
Dead leaves upon the stream
    And dead leaves on the air.

Vox Corporis

The beast to the beast is calling,
    And the soul bends down to wait;
Like the stealthy lord of the jungle,
    The white man calls his mate.

The beast to the beast is calling,
    They rush through the twilight sweet,
But the soul is a wary hunter,
    He will not let them meet.

A Ballad of Two Knights

Two knights rode forth at early dawn
    A-seeking maids to wed,
Said one, "My lady must be fair,
    With gold hair on her head."

Then spake the other knight-at-arms:
    "I care not for her face,
But she I love must be a dove
    For purity and grace."

And each knight blew upon his horn
    And went his separate way,
And each knight found a lady-love
    Before the fall of day.

But she was brown who should have had
    The shining yellow hair—
I ween the knights forgot their words
    Or else they ceased to care.

For he who wanted purity
    Brought home a wanton wild,
And when each saw the other knight
    I ween that each knight smiled.

Christmas Carol

The kings they came from out the south,
    All dressed in ermine fine,
They bore Him gold and chrysoprase,
    And gifts of precious wine.

The shepherds came from out the north,
    Their coats were brown and old,
They brought Him little new-born lambs—
    They had not any gold.

The wise-men came from out the east,
    And they were wrapped in white;
The star that led them all the way
    Did glorify the night.

The angels came from heaven high,
    And they were clad with wings;
And lo, they brought a joyful song
    The host of heaven sings.

The kings they knocked upon the door,
    The wise-men entered in,
The shepherds followed after them
    To hear the song begin.

And Mary held the little child
    And sat upon the ground;
She looked up, she looked down,
    She looked all around.

The angels sang thro' all the night
    Until the rising sun,
But little Jesus fell asleep
    Before the song was done.

THE FAERY FOREST

The faery forest glimmered
    Beneath an ivory moon,
The silver grasses shimmered
    Against a faery tune.

Beneath the silken silence
    The crystal branches slept,
And dreaming thro' the dew-fall
    The cold white blossoms wept.

A Fantasy

Her voice is like clear water
    That drips upon a stone
In forests far and silent
    Where Quiet plays alone.

Her thoughts are like the lotus
    Abloom by sacred streams
Beneath the temple arches
    Where Quiet sits and dreams.

Her kisses are the roses
    That glow while dusk is deep
In Persian garden closes
    Where Quiet falls asleep.

A Minuet of Mozart's

Across the dimly lighted room
    The violin drew wefts of sound,
    Airily they wove and wound
And glimmered gold against the gloom.

I watched the music turn to light,
    But at the pausing of the bow,
    The web was broken and the glow
Was drowned within the wave of night.

TWILIGHT

Dreamily over the roofs
    The cold spring rain is falling,
Out in the lonely tree
    A bird is calling, calling.

Slowly over the earth
    The wings of night are falling;
My heart like the bird in the tree
    Is calling, calling, calling.

THE PRAYER

My answered prayer came up to me,
    And in the silence thus spake he:
"O you who prayed for me to come,
    Your greeting is but cold and dumb."

My heart made answer: "You are fair,
    But I have prayed too long to care.
Why came you not when all was new,
    And I had died for joy of you."

Two Songs for a Child

I

Grandfather's Love

They said he sent his love to me,
    They wouldn't put it in my hand,
And when I asked them where it was
    They said I couldn't understand.

I thought they must have hidden it,
    I hunted for it all the day,
And when I told them so at night
    They smiled and turned their heads away.

They say that love is something kind,
    That I can never see or touch.
I wish he'd sent me something else,
    I like his cough-drops twice as much.

II

The Kind Moon

I think the moon is very kind
    To take such trouble just for me.
He came along with me from home
    To keep me company.

He went as fast as I could run;
    I wonder how he crossed the sky?
I'm sure he hasn't legs and feet
    Or any wings to fly.

Yet here he is above their roof;
    Perhaps he thinks it isn't right
For me to go so far alone,
    Tho' mother said I might.

ON THE TOWER

Under the leaf of many a Fable lies the Truth for those who look for it.

—Jami

On the Tower

(A play in one act.)

The Knight.
The Lady.

Voices of men and women on the ground at the foot of the tower.
The voice of the Knight's Page.

The top of a high battlemented tower of a castle. A stone ledge, which serves as a seat, extends part way around the parapet.
    Small clouds float by in the blue sky, and occasionally a swallow passes.
    Entrance R. from an unseen stairway which is supposed to extend around the outside of the tower.

THE LADY (*unseen*): Oh do not climb so fast, for I am faint
    With looking down the tower to where the earth
    Lies dreaming in the sun. I fear to fall.
THE KNIGHT (*unseen*): Lean on me, love, my love, and look not down.
L.: Call me not "love," call me your conquered foe,
    That now, since you have battered down her gates,
    Gives you the keys that lock the highest tower
    And mounts with you to prove her homage true;
    Oh bid me go no farther lest I fall,
    My foot has slipped upon the rain-worn stones,
    Why are the stairs so narrow and so steep?
    Let us go back, my lord.
K.: Are you afraid,
    Who were so dauntless till the walls gave way?
    Courage, my sweet. I would that I could climb
    A thousand times by wind-swept stairs like these,
    That lead so near to heaven.
L.: Sir, you may,
    You are a knight and very valorous;
    I am a woman. I shall never come
    This way but once.
(*The Knight and the Lady appear on the top of the tower*)

K.: Kiss me at last, my love.

L.: Oh, my sweet lord, I am too tired to kiss.
    Look how the earth is like an emerald,
    With rivers veined and flawed with fallow fields.

K. (*Lifting her veil*): Then I kiss you, a thousand thousand kisses
    For all the days ere I had won to you
    Beyond the walls and gates you barred so close.
    Call me at last your love, your castle's lord.

L. (*After a pause*): I love you.

(*She kisses him. Her veil blows away like a white butterfly over the parapet.
Faint cries and laughter from men and women under the tower*)

MEN AND WOMEN: The veil, the lady's veil!

(*The knight takes the lady in his arms*)

L.: My lord, I pray you loose me from your arms
    Lest that my people see how much we love.

K.: May they not see us? All of them have loved.

L.: But you have been an enemy, my lord,
    With walls between us and with moss-grown moats,
    Now on a sudden must I kiss your mouth?
    I who was taught before I learned to speak
    That all my house was hostile unto yours,
    Now can I put my head against your breast
    Here in the sight of all who choose to come?

K.: Are we not past the caring for their eyes
    And nearer to the heaven than to earth?
    Look up and see.

L.: I only see your face.

(*She touches his hair with her hands. Murmuring under the tower*)

K.: Why came we here in all the noon-day light
    With only darting swallows over us
    To make a speck of darkness on the sun?
    Let us go down where walls will shut us round.
    Your castle has a hundred quiet halls,
    A hundred chambers, where the shadows lie
    On things put by, forgotten long ago.
    Forgotten lutes with strings that Time has slackened,
    We two shall draw them close and bid them sing—
    Forgotten games, forgotten books still open
    Where you had laid them by at vesper-time,

And your embroidery, whereon half-worked
Weeps Amor wounded by a rose's thorn.
Shall I not see the room in which you slept,
Palpitant still and breathing of your thoughts,
Where maiden dreams adown the ways of sleep
Swept noiselessly with damosels and knights
To tourneys where the trumpet made no sound,
Blow as he might, the scarlet trumpeter,
And were the dreams not sometimes brimmed with tears
That waked you when the night was loneliest?
Will you not bring me to your oratory
Where prayers arose like little birds set free
Still upward, upward without sound of flight?
Shall I not find your turrets toward the north,
Where you defied white winter armed for war;
Your southern casements where the sun blows in
Between the leaf-bent boughs the wind has lifted?
Shall we not see the sunrise toward the east,
Watch dawn by dawn the rose of day unfolding
Its golden-hearted beauty sovereignly;
And toward the west look quietly at evening?
Shall I not see all these and all your treasures?
In carven coffers hidden in the dark
Have you not laid a sapphire lit with flame
And amethysts set round with deep-wrought gold,
Perhaps a ruby?
L.: All my gems are yours
    And all my chambers curtained from the sun.
    My lord shall see them all, in time, in time.
(*The sun begins to sink*)
K.: Shall I not see them now? Today, tonight?
L.: How could I show you in one day, my lord,
    My castle and my treasures and my tower?
    Let all the days to come suffice for this
    Since all the past days made them what they are.
    You will not be impatient, my sweet lord.
    Some of the halls have long been locked and barred,
    And some have secret doors and hard to find
    Till suddenly you touch them unawares,

And down a sable way runs silver light.
We two will search together for the keys,
But not today. Let us sit here today,
Since all is yours and always will be yours.

(*The stars appear faintly one by one*)

K. (*After a pause*): I grow a little drowsy with the dusk.

L. (*Singing*): There was a man that loved a maid,
    (Sleep and take your rest)
    Over her lips his kiss was laid,
    Over her heart, his breast.

(*The knight sleeps*)

    All of his vows were sweet to hear,
    Sweet was his kiss to take;
    Why was her breast so quick to fear,
    Why was her heart, to break?

    Why was the man so glad to woo?
    (Sleep and take your rest)
    Why were the maiden's words so few—

(*She sees that he is asleep, and slipping off her long cloak-like outer garment, she pillows his head upon it against the parapet, and half kneeling at his feet she sings very softly:*)

    I love you, I love you, I love you,
    I am the flower at your feet,
    The birds and the stars are above you,
    My place is more sweet.

    The birds and the stars are above you,
    They envy the flower in the grass,
    For I, only I, while I love you
    Can die as you pass.

(*Light clouds veil the stars, growing denser constantly. The castle bell rings for vespers, and rising, the lady moves to a corner of the parapet and kneels there*)

L.: Ave Maria! gratia plena, Dominus—

Voice of the Page (*from the foot of the tower*): My lord, my lord, they call for you at court!

(*The knight wakes. It is now quite dark*)

There is a tourney toward; your enemy

Has challenged you. My lord, make haste to come!

(*The knight rises and gropes his way toward the stairs*)

K.: I will make haste. Await me where you are.

(*To himself*)

There was a lady on this tower with me—

(*He glances around hurriedly but does not see her in the darkness*)

PAGE: My lord has far to ride before the dawn!

K. (*To himself*): Why should I tarry?

(*To the page*)

Bring my horse and shield!

(*He descends. As the noise of his footfall on the stairs dies away, the lady gropes toward the stairway, then turns suddenly, and going to the ledge where they have sat, she throws herself over the parapet*)

CURTAIN

A Note About the Author

Sara Teasdale (1884–1933) was an American poet. Born in St. Louis, Missouri, Teasdale suffered from poor health as a child before entering school at the age of ten. In 1904, after graduating from Hosmer Hall, Teasdale joined the group of female artists known as The Potters, who published *The Potter's Wheel*, a monthly literary and visual arts magazine, from 1904 to 1907. With her first two collections—*Sonnets to Duse and Other Poems* (1907) and *Helen of Troy and Other Poems* (1911)—Teasdale earned a reputation as a gifted lyric poet from critics and readers alike. In 1916, following the publication of her bestselling *Rivers to the Sea* (1915), she moved to New York City with her husband Ernst Filsinger. There, she won the 1918 Pulitzer Prize for *Love Songs* (1917), her fourth collection. Frustrated with Filsinger's prolonged absences while traveling for work, she divorced him in 1929 and moved to another apartment in the Upper West Side. Renewing her friendship with poet Vachel Lindsay, she continued to write and publish poems until her death by suicide in 1933.

A Note from the Publisher

Spanning many genres, from non-fiction essays to literature classics to children's books and lyric poetry, Mint Edition books showcase the master works of our time in a modern new package. The text is freshly typeset, is clean and easy to read, and features a new note about the author in each volume. Many books also include exclusive new introductory material. Every book boasts a striking new cover, which makes it as appropriate for collecting as it is for gift giving. Mint Edition books are only printed when a reader orders them, so natural resources are not wasted. We're proud that our books are never manufactured in excess and exist only in the exact quantity they need to be read and enjoyed.

Discover more of your favorite classics with Bookfinity™.

- Track your reading with custom book lists.
- Get great book recommendations for your personalized Reader Type.
- Add reviews for your favorite books.
- AND MUCH MORE!

Visit **bookfinity.com** and take the fun Reader Type quiz to get started.

Enjoy our classic and modern companion pairings!

Printed in the USA
CPSIA information can be obtained
at www.ICGtesting.com
JSHW080002150824
68134JS00021B/2228

9 781513 295930